Three Peaks:

A Model for Understanding Truth

Sufi George
(George Arthur Lareau)

SUFI GEORGE BOOKS
TUCSON

ISBN 1-885570-14-7

Sufi George Books: http://sgbooks.sufigeorge.net

Table of Contents

The Three Peaks Model for Understanding Truth

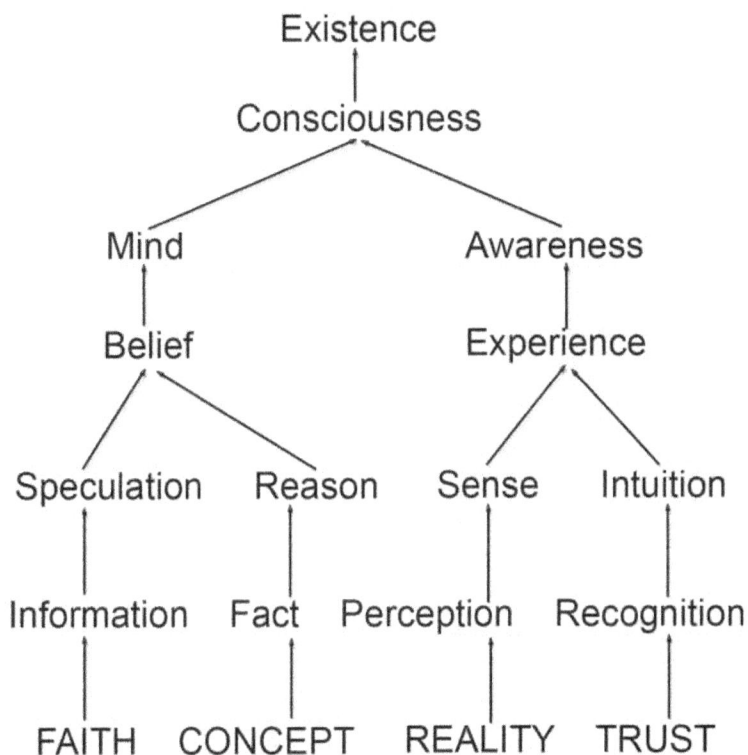

Existence
|
Consciousness

Mind   Awareness
| |
Belief   Experience

Speculation   Reason   Sense   Intuition

Information   Fact   Perception   Recognition

FAITH   CONCEPT   REALITY   TRUST

Chapter 1, Understanding Truth in the New Age

For thirty-five years, I have been a seeker of truth. I have believed and disbelieved, learned and unlearned, experimented and experienced, and all of these with great waves of energy. What I have to say is the current result of this effort.

My message is new. P. D. Ouspensky once pointed out the extreme difficulty of communicating something new because of our strong tendency to evaluate the new in terms of what we already understand-the old. I am asking you to suspend, for the moment, what you already understand.

My message consists of a new and distinctly American understanding of what truth is, how truth is created, how truth creates reality, and how we can arrive at a high level of truth that we can agree upon as a national, perhaps even as a world, community.

This is the goal of the New Age movement-world community. Yet, it seems to me that there has been little understanding of what this is or how it is to be actually accomplished.

Community is based on common-shared-truth. Alienation is based on individual truth that conflicts with that of the community. The immediate benefit to the individual that common truth provides is resolution of this conflict and dissolution of the state of alienation.

Conflict in truth separates us from each other. The achievement of world community must presume the resolution of such conflict. Conflict in general is conflict in truth, and it is changes in truth that must provide the resolution of conflict. What is called for, then, is a system of truth that can be accepted and agreed upon by everyone.

Such a system of truth need not be all-inclusive, but should freely provide for individualism. Such a truth system must not exert power over people by dictating what they must think or how they must conduct their lives.

Most acceptable would be a truth system that encourages individualism and free expression. The common elements of such a truth system must be in the foundations of our lives rather than in the expressions of our lives. Free expression based on a common consciousness of maximum truth--this is the truth system which I am presenting.

A popular New Age teaching is that we create our own reality. There have been explanations of how this is accomplished, yet I believe that my explanation is the clearest I have encountered.

World community is not achievable by governments or institutions. This reality can be accomplished only by individuals who are in control of their own realities and therefore are able to create the world reality cooperatively. The idea of creating our own reality hints at the practical value of a truth system.

With a common truth system, we can cooperatively create realities previously undreamed of. Such an approach is required to cooperatively create the New Age as visualized by the New Age movement. I present this work as a contribution to New Age thought. My reasons for doing so are based on my sense of affiliation with the New Age movement and my understanding of its purpose.

I understand that the movement intends to usher in a New Age of elevated consciousness that can establish a common bond among all people. I believe that this work contains an understanding of truth that can enable the creation of that common bond.

I refer to the truth system under discussion as the Three Peaks model, because it has three peaks and those peaks are significant in several ways.

The Three Peaks model presents four patterns by which truth is created. Together, these four patterns include all possibilities for creation of truth in human consciousness. By studying the patterns, we learn how to manage the process of truth creation. Without such management, the processes create a variety of truths which makes it impossible to experience truth in common.

The opportunity to manage truth creation presents surprising potentials. Because truth is reality, as we shall see, we can manage reality by managing truth. I am not presenting new truth, but new understanding. I am not asking you to believe what I say, but to understand it.

There is no scarcity of truth or of belief in humanity. The opposite is true--there is a bewildering amount of truth and belief. What I have searched for, and believe I have found, is a means of understanding that makes sense to Americans.

We have had many opportunities to develop understanding based on systems derived from other countries and other times, and these are not at all fully successful in America. The American mind is unique in history, and requires a system for understanding truth that is based on the American mind and the American culture.

I describe the components and dynamics of consciousness from my own authority, which is derived from thirty-five years of careful observation of my own consciousness, extensive reading and diligent personal testing of what I have read, and an unrelenting curiosity about what makes the people I meet function the way they do.

I begin my discussion of the Three Peaks model with an explanation of the words that are used. Each word is defined and explained. Once the word has been defined, it appears capitalized. If you have any doubt about the meaning of a capitalized word, please review the definition before continuing.

The words are ordinary words and the definitions are ordinary dictionary definitions, but the discussion that results is new and the reward of understanding it depends entirely on your understanding of the words used.

Chapter 2, The Words We Will Use

To help assure that we communicate, I will carefully define each word I use in the Three Peaks model, using American dictionary definitions. The words we use are probably our best-established area of common experience.

The words we use in the Three Peaks model are words that are often used carelessly. Before I checked the definitions, I used them carelessly. The words relate to nonmaterial ideas, and in casual conversation this can lead to misuse. Misuse of words leads to a lack of communication. This is not a casual conversation. Here, we will define our words very carefully.

The words are all ordinary words, using the dictionary definitions that are appropriate to this context. In that sense, there is nothing new here. The words are common and the definitions are commonly accepted. But the result is quite new.

Summary of Our Words

Existence is "state, fact or continuance of being." Being is "that which is." EXISTENCE IS THAT WHICH IS.

Consciousness is "the part of a person's mental activity of which the person is fully aware at any given time and which makes it possible to know or feel that something is or was happening or existing." CONSCIOUSNESS IS AWARE OF THAT WHICH EXISTS.

Mind is "the thinking or perceiving part of consciousness; intellect or intelligence." MIND CREATES BELIEF.

Belief is "the mental acceptance of an idea or conclusion as true, whether based on reasoning, prejudice or authority." BELIEF IS MENTAL TRUTH.

Speculation is "reasoning on the basis of incomplete or uncertain evidence." SPECULATION IS CHILDISH THINKING.

Information is "ideas gathered in any way and which are not necessarily valid." INFORMATION IS UNRELIABLE.

Reason is "a logical sequence of thought starting with what is known or assumed and advancing through inferences to a definite conclusion." REASON IS CORRECT THOUGHT.

Fact is "[ideas of] that which has been or is in reality, actuality and truth." FACT IS MENTAL REALITY.

Awareness is "having knowledge of something through alertness in observing." AWARENESS OBSERVES.

Experience is "an actual living through an event or events; personally understanding or observing something or things in general as they occur." EXPERIENCE IS OBSERVABLE.

Sense is "the faculty of receiving impressions [perceptions] through specific bodily organs and the nerves associated with them." SENSE RECEIVES PERCEPTIONS.

Perception is "awareness of objects or other data through the medium of senses." PERCEPTION IS SENSORY AWARENESS.

Intuition is "the immediate knowing of learning of something without the conscious use of reasoning." INTUITION IS KNOWING.

Recognition is "to acknowledge the existence, validity or genuineness of." RECOGNITION IS ACKNOWLEDGEMENT.

Existence. At the top of the Three Peaks model is the word "existence." Existence is "state, fact or continuance of being." Being is "that which is." EXISTENCE IS THAT WHICH IS.

Chapter 3, Existence

If something is, it has Existence. If something has Existence, it is. The only thing this rules out is nothing itself. Everything Exists.

There is no problem with this definition until we encounter beliefs that deny Existence to things that do Exist, if only as ideas. For example, some people say there is no such thing as a ghost. Of course there is. At the least, there is the idea of a ghost, and that idea is a real idea. Everyone knows what a ghost is; if ghosts didn't have some kind of reality, they would not be among our ideas.

An idea is more than nothing and it has Existence. According to this definition, it is not possible to make a statement that begins with, "There is no such thing as...."

For many, this understanding expands the boundaries of reality, and that is one of the purposes of this discussion about Existence. The important understanding to grasp here is that absolutely everything has Existence--ideas, dreams, possibilities, as well as experience of objective realities.

We start out with Existence because we are building a foundation that is as firmly rooted in truth as we can manage to understand. From a philosophical and rational standpoint, it is impossible to prove Existence without assuming it first. From a rational standpoint, we acknowledge that Existence is an assumption.

Descartes attempted to prove Existence, reportedly by crawling into a stove and working on the problem until it was solved. He came up with the famous, "I think, therefore I exist."

Although this was accepted for a long time, it is absurd. The act of thinking assumes Existence, it does not prove it. Furthermore, the statement is totally false. It is possible to Exist without thinking.

Descartes made the error of supposing that the mind, that which thinks, is all there is to consciousness. He failed to observe that consciousness can also be aware, and that awareness does not include thinking.

This is known first-hand by anyone who has experienced an altered state of consciousness. In the altered state, the mind is not needed. The altered state, by definition, is a withdrawal of attention from the mind, a movement of the attention from the mind to awareness.

In the altered state, a person knows by direct awareness and not by thinking. So, there is another avenue to the truth of Existence and that is our direct inner experience of Existence, our awareness that we Exist. It may not be rational, but such experience is different from rationality by nature so we ought not expect experience to be rational. Only the products of reason are rational.

Our direct knowing of our own Existence establishes the truth of Existence in the only way possible. Notice that our starting point is not the result of rational process but is based on direct inner knowing. I am sure you will not find it difficult to agree that you are directly aware of your Existence, and that no words are needed to convince you of the truth of this inner knowing. It may, all the same, come as a surprise that our most basic starting point is an irrational act of intuition-direct inner knowing.

18

Chapter 4, Consciousness

Next in the Three Peaks model is the word "consciousness." Consciousness is "the part of a person's mental activity of which the person is fully aware at any given time and which makes it possible to know or feel that something is or was happening or existing." CONSCIOUSNESS IS AWARE OF THAT WHICH EXISTS.

Everything Exists. Consciousness is the means we have for knowing what Exists. Consciousness knows what Exists. The study of Consciousness has produced a general agreement that our daily experience of Consciousness is limited to only a small portion of what Exists. This limited awareness has been made evident by techniques like psychoanalysis and hypnosis, among many others, which reveal a much greater potential for awareness of things that Exist.

Names have been applied to divide Existence into categories according to their accessibility: conscious mind, subconscious mind, unconscious mind, collective unconscious, for example. These are ways of describing the limitations which restrict Consciousness in its knowing of what is.

The immediate question is, if Consciousness knows what is--all that Exists--how can it know less than that? How can it be restricted? Consciousness itself by definition cannot actually have such a restriction. Yet our experience of Consciousness is restricted.

The explanation of this puzzle is that we are looking at Consciousness in a single human; the Three Peaks model is of any single human. If each human had unrestricted Consciousness, we would all know all that is; we would all be God, one might say.

Thus, the limitation of Consciousness is what makes the human condition possible. It is probably the best description of the human condition; as humans, we have restricted Consciousness.

The characteristic of Consciousness that makes the human condition distinct is attention. Attention is the same as Consciousness, but it is a limitation of it, a limitation which permits Consciousness to focus on selected ideas and experiences as opposed to knowing everything at once.

Our individual experience of Consciousness is limited, but the limitation is a question of access. This seems completely apparent from a study of Consciousness, where many ways have been found to increase such access.

Experiments in hypnosis have established that each of us has a perfect detailed memory of our life experience. Hypnosis is an altered state of consciousness, using awareness rather than mind. This suggests that the development of awareness offers potentials that can expand the experience of being human, by providing increased access to Consciousness.

Truth is "the quality of being in accordance with experience, facts or reality." In order to distinguish between Consciousness itself which has a full awareness of everything that exists, and human Consciousness which is restricted, we will refer to unrestricted Consciousness as Universal Consciousness, and to human Consciousness simply as Consciousness.

Universal Consciousness knows Truth. It knows everything-what we can call ultimate truth. Consciousness knows truth. Our Consciousness is not different from Universal Consciousness. There is only one kind of Consciousness. We can refer to human Consciousness separately, but we are only describing the limited access to Consciousness that is characteristic of the human condition.

We will be looking at the factors that ordinarily prevent our Consciousness from enjoying that potential, and the techniques for increasing our access to that potential.

Because of access limitations, truth varies from one individual to the next. Thus, truth as known by a human is relative to the individual. This condition of limited access to the truth in Consciousness and the resulting variety of truths that are created by individuals is specific to the human condition, and while it is often viewed as a handicap, it is in fact the only opportunity available for Universal Consciousness to enjoy a break from its omniscience.

The human condition provides Universal Consciousness with an opportunity to experience phenomena individually and separately, and to create truth that never Existed before. The human condition is, therefore, a massive and complex creation of Universal Consciousness designed to increase itself.

As humans, we have a different perspective on the matter, and often feel like the human condition is undesirable. In particular, we view the problems of being human as undesirable, rather than as exciting opportunities for new experiences. This perspective can be improved upon by increasing our awareness of Consciousness at least to the extent that we know what we are doing here in humanity.

Our focus in this work is on the human condition, a condition in which four creative patterns create truth which is in at least some small respect unique to the individual. Our discussion will place Universal Consciousness into the background as we examine the lives we are living here now.

Truth is relative to the individual. This does not mean that truth is not truth. It means that truth is different for different people. Truth is what Consciousness knows, and if Consciousness knows it, it is truth.

Think about the things you know to be true. Certainly, you may have doubts about many things, but there are certain things that you know are true.

It may be true to you that the earth is round. While this truth is shared by many people, there are people who still hold the truth that the earth is flat. Before Copernicus 300 years ago, everyone knew that the earth was flat. This well-established truth, then, can be seen for what it is-relative to the individual.

It is easy to identify our truth because it is our truth that makes us tell another person that he or she is wrong. If we have doubt, we consider the other person's viewpoint; if we have truth, the other person is wrong. It seldom occurs to us that the other person also has truth.

If someone else tells you that you are wrong, then that person makes the statement based on his or her truth. Every time such a conflict occurs, it is proof that truth is relative to the individual.

Truth is the final result in the Three Peaks model. The model illustrates how truth is created in Consciousness. And as long as we are talking about Consciousness that is limited, and about limitations that are not uniform among humans, and about processes that can produce infinite combinations--all demonstrated by the Three Peaks model--we are talking about truth that varies among individuals.

My truth, your truth, is truth. Each and every one of us knows what is true, based on our beliefs and our experiences. In many cases, we become completely convinced about what is true. It is only those people who are in a state of conflict and confusion who do not have a firm sense of truth.

We have difficulty acknowledging the different truth of someone else, however. Our conviction about our truth seems to demand, in many cases, that we consider conflicting truths of others as untruth. The Three Peaks helps resolve this problem by enabling us to understand that everyone's truth is genuine truth, in spite of its uniqueness.

Truth is not only relative to the individual; it is also relative to the development of the individual. Truth changes in specific individuals. As our beliefs change, as our experience increases, our truth changes.

In many cases where our truth conflicts with the truth of someone else, that conflict is resolved. Resolution means that one of us has changed our truth so that it agrees with the other truth. Whichever one of us experienced a change in truth proved that truth is relative to the development of the individual.

Because humans develop, there is usually truth in the process of being formed, truth not yet truth, truth about which we are still wondering. That is doubt, and is not the final product that we are discussing. We are talking about truth that is created and accepted as truth and about which we are convinced.

Truth is "the quality of being in accordance with experience, facts or reality." Experience never stops; facts are constantly being identified; reality is constantly being discovered. At any given point, truth is the best that we have done; but it is always changing.

Truth is not a final destination, until our truth coincides with the truth of Universal Consciousness.

In the human condition, Consciousness has two apparent aspects: mind and awareness. These two aspects collect truth from the four patterns that create it.

Chapter 5, Mind

At this point, the Three Peaks model divides into two branches. One leads to mind, the other to awareness.

Mind is "the thinking or perceiving part of consciousness; intellect or intelligence." Thinking is "using the mind for arriving at conclusions, making decisions, drawing inferences, etc."

Thinking is the mind at work creating truth-- conclusions, decisions. When the mind arrives at a conclusion or a decision, that result is accepted by Consciousness as truth.

Mind has the unique ability to process ideas. An idea is "a mental image, anything existing in the mind as an object of knowledge or thought." Ideas are things that can Exist only in the mind, and they are the only things that Exist in the mind.

Some ideas become conclusions in the form of belief. Belief is "the mental acceptance of an idea or conclusion as true, whether based on reasoning, prejudice or authority."

Belief can be scientific knowledge or it can be fantasy. It can be anything in between. Belief is simply what the Mind accepts as truth, regardless how it is created. If you believe something, it is as true as truth can be.

We know first-hand that ideas can be communicated and it is perhaps safe to estimate that most are received by communication as ideas which already Existed in other human Minds. Other ideas "pop" into the Mind; when such ideas make their first appearance in a human Mind, they are from the only possible source, Universal Consciousness that knows everything.

Our definition of Mind emphasizes the truth that results from the thinking taking place in the Mind. What Consciousness receives through Mind it accepts as truth, unless it conflicts with what it receives from awareness, its connection with experience.

These are the two ways a human Consciousness receives its truth--Mind and awareness. These encompass everything that happens in our Mind and everything that occurs in our experience. That doesn't leave anything out. The word for the truth created by Mind is belief. BELIEF IS MENTAL TRUTH.

Belief and truth are the same thing in Mind. A Belief is true, by definition. Truth is more than Belief, however, for it also includes experience, as we shall see.

We are aware that Belief varies among individuals. With the understanding that Belief is truth to the Mind aspect of Consciousness, we can understand that each variation of Belief among people is the sincere and valid truth of the individual.

It also gives us the insight that our own truth is itself a variation. We can reduce the amount of conflict that we experience from the varying truth that different people have by realizing that our truth is only one more relative variation. We can realize that in the human condition there is only the best that we can do which is what each of us is already doing.

Relative truth is not worth fighting over. Fighting assumes that we're done creating our truth, that we've arrived at the final stage of truth. There is no such stage in the human condition, as we have seen, because truth keeps changing relative to the development of the individual. Fighting in defense of our truth is an admission that we have tried to stop our development.

We will be discussing the idea of maximum truth, the highest truth that a human can create. Maximum truth is still a truth that is relative to the human condition, but it is as far as we can go with the creation of truth as humans.

That does not mean that maximum truth does not change; it does. It changes as we make progress in the ways we create it. I have introduced several kinds of truth. Universal Consciousness knows ultimate truth--everything there is to know about everything. Human consciousness knows relative truth, truth that is relative to individuals. Maximum truth is the best truth that humanity can create for itself, although it is relative to our improving ability to create it.

I will also refer to absolute truth; this is truth that people attempt to protect from change, usually by reinforcement, and is symptomatic of a refusal to grow. The sources of Belief can be, by definition, reasoning, prejudice and authority.

Prejudice--prejudgment, or forming a judgment before all the facts are in--and authority--dogma--belong to the pattern called Faith in the Three Peaks model.

As we discuss the four patterns, we are pretending that each pattern operates separately. This pretense is only to allow us to examine each pattern in some detail. In fact, all four patterns operate simultaneously with varying degrees of emphasis and coordination.

Further, each pattern is discussed in terms of its extreme or maximum capacity, to highlight that capacity; in fact, the patterns are heavily involved in various stages of creation of truth and produce final truth after considerable activity in those stages.

Chapter 6, The Faith Pattern

Faith is "the complete, blind acceptance of something, especially something not supported by reason."

In the Faith pattern, speculation is applied to information, resulting in Belief.

Speculation is "reasoning on the basis of incomplete or uncertain evidence." During childhood, we form Belief about every issue that comes up. There is no assurance during childhood that the Information we have available to us is valid. Nor have we yet reached the age where we have learned to employ that formal, scientific discipline called reason. The best we can do as children is speculation. SPECULATION IS CHILDISH THINKING.

Information is "ideas gathered in any way and which are not necessarily valid." INFORMATION IS UNRELIABLE.

The Belief we form during childhood, then, very likely suffers from lack of fact and lack of disciplined reasoning. Such truth should be reevaluated in adulthood.

As a four-year-old, I was taught by a mischievous tenant that all books have sixteen chapters. He showed me such a book as proof. That was truth to me for several years. I recall my chagrin when I learned that this truth was not supported by the books in the school library.

At first, I thought something was wrong with the books, though, not with my truth. Then my truth changed, and I felt like a fool. I was--I had been fooled.

As children, we are taught that truth changes. Santa Claus and the Tooth Fairy and the Easter Bunny all fade into myth as it is discovered that these truths are not reinforced by the larger community. Such Belief is initially promoted by the child's family, and as the child's community enlarges to include outside acquaintances the child discovers that reinforcement is not available.

When confronted by this discovery, the family ceases its reinforcement as well. At this point, truth changes and the child feels like a fool. With such illuminating experiences in childhood, it is surprising that many people still expect truth to stand still--to be absolute.

It may be that the fear of feeling like a fool plays a large role in our resistance to examining our truths. The reinforcement factor is important to recognize when discussing Belief created by Speculation; some childhood Belief is carried into adulthood by means of continued reinforcement.

Particularly in cases where people suffer because of their particular truth, it can be helpful to examine the influence that reinforcement has in maintaining childhood truth intact into adulthood.

The most visible reinforcement system for maintaining childish Belief in adulthood is dogma. Dogma is "belief or opinion handed down by authority as true and indisputable and usually arbitrary or arrogant."

Dogma appears to involve extension of one's community into the past. This inclusion of the past may be a reinforcement against influences in the present which cause a conflict in truth.

An example of dogma is that, by and large, we believe in common is that criminals should be punished for their crimes. This is an age-old idea that has been handed down generation to generation. It is an Old Testament idea. While the New Testament attempted to recreate God as a God of love as opposed to the old Testament God of wrath, the belief that criminals should be punished continues to hold on as dogma.

From our discussion to this point, it is clear that criminals are people who behave according to their truth, as we all do. We would not want to be punished because of the particular truth we hold; why do we punish the criminal just because his truth is different? The criminal is doing exactly what we are doing-living according to truth.

The punishment is an attempt to resolve this conflict in truth, because the conflict disturbs our community. Punishment, though, is completely irrelevant to resolution of that conflict. If we are to solve the problem, we need to change the truth of the criminal. The truth of the criminal is clearly based on childhood belief. As we will see, the adult who reasons participates in community, must participate in community, because reason itself is what creates community, and is itself a community product and process.

Reasoning leads to community; speculation leads to alienation. The criminal experiences alienation from the community; therefore his or her Belief is based on the Faith pattern of childhood.

The problem of crime is a community problem. The truth of the criminal was created as highly individualized Speculative Belief. This means the criminal was alienated from the community by conflict with the Reasoned truth of the community. The community had the opportunity to resolve the conflict and assist the criminal in developing Reasoned Belief that was cooperative with the community, but it did not do so.

Perhaps the education system failed in this case, perhaps the people around the criminal failed. It is also unlikely that the criminal's Beliefs would have been created if there had not been influence from his limited community which reinforced certain truths.

Community, then, created the criminal by failure and negligence, and the criminal is the victim. Dogma makes us punish the victim instead of changing the truth of the segment of the community responsible.

As we will see, this question of changing someone else's truth is a right of the community. The greater the variety of truth in individuals, the less well the community functions. This is because varying truths create conflict and conflict is the opposite of community.

In order to preserve and promote community, the community must work toward certain common truths within the community in order to eliminate conflict. This is an explosive issue, however. Hitler tried to change the truth of the community, and we don't like what happened.

In America, we treasure our personal independence from exactly that kind of tyranny. However grand the concept of a community without conflict may be, our various experiments in creating such Utopias have failed. I remind you, then, that I am leading up to a concept of community that is based on only one shared truth--maximum truth.

This cannot be the product of any individual, however tyrannical. This can only be the product of the community itself, a truth that is achieved cooperatively as the result of the best effort of all concerned.

Because maximum truth can provide a common foundation for truth, it allows for all variations in truth to spring from common roots, assuring a large measure of harmony and freedom from conflict.

The most attractive aspect of maximum truth is that it can be agreed upon. It does not require any coercion. It requires only that children grow into adults and continue growing. Children become physical adults, but do not in all cases learn to reason. In such cases, their truth continues to be created by the Faith pattern through Speculation on Information.

Of course, there are all gradations of people between those who have not learned to reason and those who have refined it into an art.

In childhood, there is less consequence to changes in truth than there is in adulthood because adults are expected to behave with an acceptable measure of consistency. Children can be inconsistent, responding to changing truth, and it is termed growth.

There is in America an assumption that adults do not need to continue the growth process, and this assumption Exists as a Belief in consistent behavior which is given a large amount of social reinforcement. This assumption has the character of dogma about it.

Perhaps it develops from our need for consistent support from our parents when we are children. While that is important to us as children, it is a handicap to us as adults.

True consistency calls for absolute truth, and as we have seen, this is not the nature of truth because truth is relative and changing.

Motherhood is an example of a truth that demands consistency of many women. Children need mothers, but once the children are grown into adults themselves, the need changes. In many cases, the truth does not; the mother may continue behaving consistently as a mother, perpetuating a set of behaviors that become increasingly less relevant to reality.

Many mothers experience severe crisis when their children "leave the nest" because they are not prepared to change their truth. They believe in the dogma of consistency in adult behavior, and this makes them suffer.

I have led a remarkably inconsistent life and it has enabled me to exercise great freedom in the management of my truth. I have nothing to say in support of consistency for its own sake.

In the Three Peaks model, the Faith pattern creates childish Belief by applying Speculation to Information.

Chapter 7, The Concept Pattern

Reason is "a logical sequence of thought starting with what is known or assumed and advancing through inferences to a definite conclusion." Logic is "the science of correct reasoning and valid thought." REASON IS CORRECT THOUGHT.

Reason relies on fact. Fact is "[ideas of] that which has been or is in reality, actuality and truth." FACT IS MENTAL REALITY. The scientific process for establishing Fact is a process of agreement. No private, isolated instance of something establishes a Fact. Before something can become a Fact, it must be shared among people, preferably a substantial majority of people qualified to assess it.

For example, no experimental result is accepted as Fact in the scientific community until others have been able to perform the experiment with the same result. This reveals the primary distinction between Belief created by Speculation and Belief created by Reason. It is regularly overlooked because of its transparency.

Speculative Belief does not rely on the majority community. It can be highly individualized, even entirely personal. Because it does not require consensus from the community in the way that Fact requires, Speculative Belief can alienate the believer from the community through conflict and lack of consensus.

The opposite occurs in the case of Reasoned Belief. Because Reason depends on Fact which by definition requires consensus of the community, and because Reason itself is a creation of the community that is used in common, the person with Reasoned Belief experiences a large sense of community.

Truth that resides in Consciousness as Reasoned Belief is truth shared by the larger community. Because Reason is disciplined, exactly the same truths can be held in common, as ideas created by a process identical in each individual.

Reason does not work perfectly because not all people learn it perfectly; but potentially it has the power to unite people in common truth, and in actual operation the majority community in America enjoys substantial common truth based on Reasoned Belief.

This is the Concept pattern for creating truth, in which Belief is created by Reason applied to Fact. The Belief created by the Concept pattern is not "more true" than Belief created by the Faith pattern; but it enables the believer to experience a larger amount of community.

There is an implicit weakness present here that should be observed. Fact, before it achieves consensus, is not Fact. After consensus, it is Fact. Yet it has not changed in any way. As Reason advances, Fact can once again lose consensus in favor of some new Fact. Fact, then, is not ultimate truth, it is consensus; and that consensus changes.

Since Fact is the foundation for Reason, the truth of Reason is not ultimate. It is impressive, but its primary value is not in its reliability but in its consensus--its community.

I am saying that it does not matter so much exactly what the truth is that we agree upon; more important is that we agree on it.

Truth is relative anyway, and changes. We cannot hope for absolute truth except by an artificial stunting of our growth. It is never truth itself that causes conflict, but rather our defense of variations in truth. Resolution of conflict is more valuable to us than which truth wins.

Our ability to have a sense of community depends entirely on our ability to share truth. If my truth were different from everyone else's truth, I would have no community at all; I would experience total alienation.

Humanity has done a wonderful thing in creating Reason. Reason enables us to share common truth on a large scale. Without Reason, we would still be a globe of warring tribes, each alienated from the rest, each experiencing conflict with the rest. With Reason, we have a system for thinking.

Thinking need not produce the random results of personal Speculation. We can agree on exactly how to think, and we can think exactly the same things. Having this kind of experience in common has enabled us to commune, communicate, have community.

Again, it does not matter so much what we think. It is the fact that we are able to do it together that is significant. This is what has made it possible for us to have such a thing as a large majority community.

We have seen that Fact is not a perfect basis for Reason, so we know that Reason is not an infallible process. Since the products of Reason keep changing, we know this anyway. Truth from Reason is still relative truth.

But Reason makes it possible to step into a world where we can share ideas with a great many others, a world where we can make individual contributions to the ongoing cooperative process of creating the reality of community, a world instead of the closet of alienation.

Curiously, we do not even have to be skilled in Reason. As long as we understand the process of Reason, we can accept the products of Reason as common truth without hav ing to duplicate the process in every instance. As long as we know that a great deal of Reason went into the project of landing a man on the moon, we can accept the truth of it.

We do not, could not, go through every step of the Reasoning that contributed to that effort. We do not confirm the Reasoning for ourselves. It is enough to have faith in Reason.

To have faith in Reason, one must know enough about Reason to understand and accept what it is and what it does. I have twice spoken with people who do not believe that we have landed a man on the moon. These are adults who have failed to learn enough about Reason, what it is and does.

It does not matter whether we have landed a man on the moon or not. What matters is that it is a truth we can hold in common, thanks to Reason and our faith in Reason. What matters is that we can experience community instead of alienation.

Community is man-made. It is created by common truth. The world's religions contributed greatly to creating community by spreading--whether by war or by teaching--their truths.

As things stand today, the world consists of several major communities with differing common truths. Communities have grown to the extent that we now have conflicts that are global in scope. There remain a number of smaller communities, in addition, but our direction is very clear as we look back over the past several thousand years. We are headed for a world community.

It is now far too late for us to change our minds about this. We are committed to the concept of community. Our only sensible efforts with regard to community, then, are in the direction of increased unity and decreased conflict.

This introduces the words used in the left half of the Three Peaks model.

Chapter 8, Awareness

Consciousness knows truth from the Belief it receives from Mind and from the experience it receives from awareness. Awareness is "having knowledge of something through alertness in observing." AWARENESS OBSERVES.

Experience is "an actual living through an event or events; personally understanding or observing something or things in general as they occur." EXPERIENCE IS OBSERVABLE.

Awareness observes Experience. It is an irrational process because it has nothing to do with Reason. Speculation and Reason may make interpretations of observed Experience, but that is a translation of Experience into ideas, the only things Mind can process. The actual observations remain non-verbal.

Awareness is not quite as easy to isolate in our Consciousness as is Mind. Mind makes a trail of words and concepts that is easy to follow. Awareness quietly collects observations of Experience, and our attention is usually on the observations themselves and not on the Awareness of them.

Awareness can observe itself, however. Emotional Experience, for example, may often bring with it an Awareness that we are observing ourselves Experiencing the emotion. Such an Experience of

Awareness may be sensed as a sudden distancing between Awareness which is observing and the part of us that is feeling the Experience.

The French existentialist philosopher Jean-Paul Sartre made a big thing out of this, identifying the ability of Awareness to be Aware of itself. While the existentialists concluded that such Awareness of Awareness meant that each human lived in sustained alienation, this was the result of studying one creative pattern only so far and ignoring the others.

The existentialists did establish well that Awareness can be Aware of itself, though, and that is important to know when we live in such ignorance of it. Awareness does not think. It is Mind that thinks. Awareness observes. We spend so much of our time in the Mind that we seldom think about Awareness.

Our overemphasis on Mind has been responsible for creating our highly scientific and technological community. It is a grand demonstration of how creative Mind can be.

But as a consequence, we have largely ignored Awareness. So little do we use Awareness that we call it by a strange name--altered state of consciousness.

Awareness observes. Mind creates mental truth through Reason or Speculation, based on Fact or Information. The truth created by Mind is always subject to change. Observation, however, can only relate to what is there, to what Exists in Experience.

Mind creates mental truth, but Awareness observes the real thing--Experience. We are aware that we Exist because we are Aware of the Experience of it. We observe it directly. We do not have to create mental truths out of ideas in order to make ourselves Exist, as Descartes thought; the truth is there for the observing.

Awareness does not literally create truth by observing; it merely collects observations that are true. But such observations introduce new truths that did not Exist in Awareness before, and the process looks like it is richly creative.

The truth that is created by Awareness changes, but this change is the result of accumulation of truth. As accumulation of observations continues, truth expands in Awareness. It does not become more true, it just becomes more.

Reason arrives at truth through a process that requires the best minds of the community working cooperatively. Even then, the truth created by Reason is never absolute.

The truth accumulated by Awareness is never ultimate because the accumulation process is ongoing, changing truth by changing how much of it there is in Awareness. But this truth is not subject to question regarding its trustworthiness. It is questionable only with regard to its completeness.

Before we explore the potential truth available through Awareness, we need to understand the sources of observable Experience. For human Consciousness, there are two sources of Experience, sense perception of objective reality, and intuitive recognition of subjective reality.

Chapter 9, The Reality Pattern

From Awareness, Consciousness receives observation of Experience, and not Experience itself. In the case of intuitive recognition, the Trust pattern, this actually becomes blurred, but this is distinctly true of sense perception.

Sense is "the faculty of receiving impressions [perceptions] through specific bodily organs and the nerves associated with them." SENSE RECEIVES PERCEPTIONS.

Perception is "awareness of objects or other data through the medium of senses." PERCEPTION IS SENSORY AWARENESS.

Consciousness itself does not Experience objective reality. It has only the Awareness of Perception received by Sense.

Perception itself is only Awareness of what the Sensory system produces. This can be readily understood by thinking about how our sensory apparatus works.

Let us use sight as our example, since it is estimated that 90% of our Sense Perceptions involve sight. My eyes Perceive light waves and translate those Perceptions into a complicated series of electrical and chemical signals which are then processed by my brain--in complete darkness.

From there, the process is less well understood but finally results in an interpretation which my Awareness observes as the Experience of light. My Awareness has never seen actual light. As far as it knows, there is an Experience which it observes through Sense Perception and it observes that Experience as light.

There is a big difference between an Experience that happens in darkness and the idea of light. The idea of light, since it is an idea, Exists in Mind, and cannot Exist in Awareness. If we leave Mind out of it, Awareness can only observe Sense Perceptions and the truth then is that there are Sense Perceptions.

It is Mind that says there is actual light, but Mind only has ideas about light, not the actual Experience. The actual Experience is of Sense Perception, not of light. Where is the light? There is no light, as far as we can know through Awareness of Sense Perception.

There is the idea of light in the Mind, but an idea of light is a mental truth, not actual light. When the idea of light from Mind combines with Awareness of Sense Perception, Consciousness has a truth called light. That truth is based on a mental truth and a nonmaterial observation process.

Where does the Sense Perception of light come from? Awareness cannot know beyond Sense Perception (in this pattern). It cannot know objective reality directly. Awareness cannot provide us with knowing that objective reality exists. It can only collect observations of Sense Perception.

If light comes from objective reality, how can we prove it? Granted, we don't normally wonder about this, but in order to understand the nature of Awareness it is a question worth wrestling with.

We cannot prove it. We have no way of directly connecting Consciousness with objective reality. Consciousness deals only with the nonmaterial--ideas from Mind and observations from Awareness. If it doesn't Exist in Consciousness, it doesn't exist, because Consciousness knows everything that Exists.

Yet it seems that Consciousness knows that objective reality Exists. The difficulty is in proving how it could know. So far, it seems that it couldn't possibly know. The only way that Consciousness could know that objective reality Exists is if Universal Consciousness made up the whole thing to begin with.

It is conceivable that objective reality exists in Consciousness itself, where it is known as truth. We would not be able to tell the difference if objective reality was "all in our minds" or if it really existed the way we think it does--unless we accumulated additional observations that made it clear that it is all in Consciousness.

A warning--this is where we're headed. Fritjof Capra, speaking of Gregory Bateson, one of our century's greatest thinkers, says, "When Bateson looked at the living world, he saw its principles of organization as being essentially mental, with mind being immanent in matter at all levels of life. He thus arrived at a unique synthesis of notions of mind with notions of matter; a synthesis that was, as he liked to point out, neither mechanical nor supernatural." from The Tao of Physics.

Geoffrey Chew, a prominent physicist, says, "I take it as obvious that the quantum principles render inevitable the idea that objective Cartesian reality is an approximation. You cannot have the principles of quantum mechanics and, at the same time, say that our ordinary ideas of external are an exact description. You can produce enough examples, showing how a system subject to quantum principles begins to exhibit classical behavior when it becomes sufficiently complex....You can actually show how classical behavior emerges as an approximation to quantum behavior."

While these quotations may take some study to be understood, they are saying that objective reality is not very objective in a material sense after all. Awareness has observation powers only, and in this pattern it observes Sense Perceptions only.

Awareness of Sense Perceptions involves a complicated sensory system that separates Awareness from objective reality. What Awareness observes is accepted in Consciousness as truth. Consciousness accepts the truth of objective reality without ever coming into direct contact with it.

In parallel with the Faith pattern that creates Speculative Belief, the Reality pattern is active during childhood. Awareness becomes filled early in life with truth based on Sense Perception. Our Experience of objective reality is childhood truth. The result of unquestioned acceptance of Sense Perception from childhood results in an objective reality that is accepted as truth.

Yet, there is no vestige of this objective reality in Awareness, only the collected Sense Perceptions. Awareness contains truth about objective reality, but it has never seen anything or touched anything directly.

It is not characteristic of childhood to question the truth of objective reality. Usually, the child is too occupied assembling the truth to question its reality. The adult has the ability to pose the question, however.

A second parallel that exists between Speculative Belief and Sense Perception is the lack of consensus, or the privacy of the created truth. No one can share another's Sense Perception.

The only way we can assume that we Experience objective reality similarly to the way other people Experience it is through the Mind. Without common ideas about it, without the ability to communicate with language and compare notes, each of us would Experience objective reality as privately as we Experience dreams.

On its own, then, Sense Perception creates an individualized truth. While Mind has enabled us to establish a high degree of consensus about objective reality, there are clear instances of Sense Perception creating truth that lacks consensus.

An example is the imaginary playmate of childhood, a person who can be seen with the eyes and related to as an objective reality. We can identify many more instances where objective reality lacks consensus; generally, we take the opposite approach, reinforcing our consensus rather than looking for instances of that consensus falling apart.

You feel an itch on your forearm. You look, and you can't see any cause for the itch. No one else can feel your itch. How do you know your itch is an objective reality? You do not know; you assume that it is. You have faith in Reason that makes you say, "Well, if I had enough Facts about the matter, then I would know the cause of my itch."

But Reason would only give you mental truth. You will never know if your Sense Perception of the itch was based on something in objective reality, or if it was "all in your mind," which is to say, in your Awareness. You cannot establish consensus about your itch. It is a completely private Experience, as is all Sense Perception.

In order to establish that your itch exists in objective reality, you need the agreement of other people. And you can't get it. Four witnesses to an accident do not agree on what happened. If we are one of the four, we think the other three are mistaken. Each has a personal set of Sense Perceptions of the accident. While there may be consensus on many of the Facts, there is a lack of consensus on many of the details.

Ten people watch an Indian fakir perform the rope trick. The fakir throws a rope into the air and it stays there. A boy climbs up. The fakir tosses a sword up. Dismembered portions of the boy tumble down. The fakir tosses them back up and the boy comes down brandishing the sword. Everyone has the same Sense Perceptions. But a movie camera photographs the rope being tossed into the air, falling to the ground, and a group of people standing motionless, watching a motionless fakir and a motionless boy.

The only explanation for the rope trick is that the Sense Perception happened in Awareness and not in objective reality. You see something; then you decide that your eyes "played a trick on you." You just experienced something in Awareness of Sense Perception that did not actually exist in objective reality.

You hear someone call your name. But there is no one there. You shrug it off. It is possible to observe that objective reality has a lot of cracks in it. Our strong tendency is to reinforce our consensus that objective reality is there in a material sense. But if we can stop that reinforcement long enough, we can observe for ourselves that it actually has some dreamlike qualities. We can see through it.

Our tendency to reinforce makes us shrug off and forget the evidence that surrounds us. If we accumulated our evidence that objective reality is not material, instead of forgetting about it, its nonmateriality would become evident to us.

"There must be a logical explanation" is our main reinforcer. Such an explanation often is not forthcoming; it is simply an exercise of our faith in Reason. We see things appear and disappear; we really do, but we shrug it off.

All you have to do is make your own observations and you will see that this is true. You may see a parking spot and head for it, only to find it already taken; but there was no other traffic. You measure the seconds of time in your mind, wondering how someone could have reached that space before you. It doesn't seem possible, but you shrug it off, saying, "There must be a logical explanation. If I knew all the Facts...."

Perhaps I can't convince you of the nonmateriality of objective reality. But your own experience can show you. Reinforce less and you will see. Objective reality can only be Experienced and that Experience is private. Ideas about objective reality can be processed by the Mind, but these are ideas, not objective reality itself. There is nothing objective about the Experience of objective reality.

Experience is not material. The act of seeing has no weight or solidity. It is only the Experience that reaches Awareness. Without such Experience, there would be no Awareness of objective reality, no inkling that there is such a thing. Sense Perception would be dead-ended if it did not connect to Awareness, and in that case objective reality would not Exist in Consciousness. Objective reality would then not Exist.

Objective reality Exists in Consciousness where it is a nonmaterial phenomenon. This is a difficult conclusion to accept because we are so convinced of the Existence of material reality. But that conviction, like the convictions of Speculative Belief, was formed in childhood and may be suspect for that reason alone. As adults, we can reconsider the conviction of childhood, just as we reconsider the Speculative

Belief we formed in childhood.

What is required is a conflict in truth, some truth that will conflict with our conviction of the materiality of objective reality. Such truth has become available from Mind in the form of discoveries by particle physicists.

Modern physics, in its exploration of the atom, has concluded that we live in a nonmaterial universe. In the 1920s, the development of quantum theory showed that atoms are not hard and indestructible but consist of vast regions of space in which extremely small particles move, and that even these particles are not material. They are very abstract entities, appearing sometimes as particles and sometimes as waves.

Fritjof Capra, a high energy physicist famous for his insights into the philosophical implications of modern science, says, "Quantum theory has...demolished the classical concepts of solid objects and of strictly deterministic laws of nature. At the subatomic level, the solid material objects of classical physics dissolve into wavelike patterns of probabilities, and these patterns, ultimately, do not represent probabilities of things, but rather probabilities of interconnections. Because of these interconnections, quantum theory reveals a basic unity of all parts of the universe. The universe cannot be taken apart into tiny bits. There are no basic building blocks in the material sense, only a complicated web of relations between the parts of the whole."

This is saying that the entire universe is a single entity, nonmaterial in nature, consist ing of a network of interrelated patterns. Physicists are people, too, and facing this discovery was no easier for them than it is for us.

Heisenberg wrote, "The violent reaction on the recent development of modern physics can only be understood when one realizes that here the foundations of physics have started moving; and that this motion has caused the feeling that the ground would be cut from science."

In his autobiography, Einstein wrote, "All my attempts to adapt the theoretical foundation of physics to this new type of knowledge failed completely. It was as if the ground had been pulled out from under one, with no firm foundation to be seen anywhere, upon which one could have built."

Neils Bohr wrote, "The great extension of our experience in recent years has brought to light the insufficiency of our simple mechanical conceptions and, as a consequence, has shaken the foundation on which the customary interpretation of observation was based. Physicists have now had time to accept the nonmateriality of the universe, and to make great progress in discovering more about it. But most of us have not yet faced this discovery."

This information from physicists is of the greatest importance. It provides us with conflict of truth on a grand scale. It is, I think, the most exciting conflict in truth that we have yet had to face.

Capra says, "The universe is no longer seen as a machine, made up of a multitude of separate objects, but appears as a harmonious indivisible whole; a network of dynamic relationships that include the human observer and his or her consciousness in an essential way. The fact that modern physics, the manifestation of an extreme specialization of the rational mind, is now making contact with mysticism, the essence of religion and manifestation of an extreme specialization of the intuitive mind, shows very beautifully the unity and complementary nature of the rational and intuitive modes of consciousness." [*The Turning Point*]

As Capra says, there is support for the startling discoveries of physics in another sector--intuition. This is our Trust pattern.

Chapter 10, The Trust Pattern

Awareness observes Experience created by two processes, Sense and intuition.

Intuition is "the immediate knowing or learning of something without the conscious use of reasoning." INTUITION IS KNOWING.

Intuition knows things because of recognition. Recognition is "to acknowledge the existence, validity or genuineness of." RECOGNITION IS ACKNOWLEDGMENT.

In this creative process, Intuition knows only what is acknowledged by Recognition. If an Experience is not acknowledged, it is not available to Intuition and becomes lost, as if it never happened. This is a feature in common with the Reality pattern, except that we have been Recognizing our Sense Perception since infancy. After so much practice at it, we call it Perception.

In the Trust pattern, we do not have the habit, and must make a point of it by calling it a different name, one which reflects the need to do what we already do with our Experience of Sense Perception--Recognize the Experience.

Recognition is different from Perception, then, only in terms of how little we use it compared to Perception.

Otherwise, it is the same thing.

Intuition is Experience, not a product of Mind. Like Sense Perception, it is a non-verbal and irrational process. It is more reliable than Sense Perception because it does not rely on a complicated system like the sensory system.

Intuition knows directly and immediately; there is nothing separating the knowing of Intuition from what it is knowing.

As we saw earlier, our only way of knowing that we Exist is through Intuition, the direct knowing that we Exist. This example of Intuition demonstrates its capacity for creating truth that is unquestionable. It is the only pattern of truth creation that has this capacity.

Speculative Belief is questionable because its truth is changeable, as is the case with Reasoned Belief. Sense Perception is questionable because it creates Experience that lacks consensus, and which, as I hope I have shown, is easy to misunderstand.

Unquestionable truth is the product of Intuition, but it must not be supposed that a little bit of Intuitive truth is enough. Each of the patterns that create truth operates within a range of trustworthiness.

Speculative Belief can have varying degrees of community, ranging from the purely private to the limited community, producing truth that lacks consensus. Reasoned Belief can be created along many lines, depending on the selection of Fact used, with a variety of results, and its truth is always subject to change. Sense Perception produces private Experience which assumes consensus only through Mind, and exceptions to that consensus can be identified, revealing the illusory nature of objective reality. Intuition creates truth according to the Recognition it has access to.

We have a full and practiced Recognition of our Existence, and that creates an ultimate truth. However, there is much Intuitive Experience that does not receive Recognition at all, or very little, in which case the truth created by Intuition suffers from inadequate detail and must be viewed as incomplete.

When Recognition is not utilized, we ignore Experience. We are ignorant. Limited Experience necessarily results in limited truth. The truth of Intuition is unquestionable, even when it is limited. If it is limited, however, it cannot have an adequate context of Experience within which its truth can have significant meaning.

Thus, even unquestionable truth is relative--relative to its own body. As this body of truth changes, which can only occur by expansion, truth assumes greater meaning and reliability.

Intuition is a capacity that requires deliberate development, parallel to the development of Reason. It is an adult capacity in America. It is active from childhood and appears to be a native capacity, but our culture intentionally ignores its development in favor of creating Experience through the other patterns.

It is often observed that children exhibit considerable Intuitive functioning, and that they are persuaded that it is not viewed by the community as an acceptable means of creating truth. If you have raised a child, you may have witnessed many such incidents.

Intuitional knowing is direct Experience without benefit of Mind or Sense. Other than our Intuitional knowing that we Exist, the most common example of direct knowing is dreaming. No Sense is involved; the dream is Experienced directly without an intervening system.

In dreams, we see without eyes and hear without ears. When we dream, we accept the dream environment as completely real. Objects in dreams are not only visible but we can sit in a dream chair without falling through it, we can touch things and feel how solid they are, we can pinch ourselves and it hurts. While we are dreaming, we are completely fooled by the reality of the dream.

Usually, it doesn't even occur to us to question the reality of a dream. We could use dream rulers to measure the lengths of dream objects, we could weigh them on dream scales, and we would have dream proof of the reality of dream objects.

Recalling our discussion of seeing light, it is interesting that we can see light in dreams where there is no light source. Realizing this helps us to understand how we can Experience light from objective reality without that light ever actually getting beyond the backs of our eyeballs.

As we dream it, the dream is truth. It is still truth when we awaken, but our Mind attacks it and sets up a barrier of ideas that persuade us that the dream was not truth. Dreams are real while they happen, but we manage to dismiss that reality when we awaken.

Intuitive Recognition of the dream Experience results in truth. There is no question that the Experience happened. It is observed by Awareness. There is no suspicion that the Experience is imperfectly observed--no process is involved to cause error in observation.

To the extent that the dream is acknowledged by Recognition, Awareness observes the truth of the Experience. Upon close observation, it may be noted that when we dream we are not as mentally alert or awake as we are during the day. Intuitively, we Recognize this difference, and it makes it easy for us to dismiss the reality of the dream.

Simply put, we aren't the same conscious self in the dream as we know ourselves to be during the day. If we could be just as awake and aware in a dream as we are now, it would be different. Then we would be able to make a direct comparison between dream reality and ordinary reality.

In fact, if we can make such a comparison, it would mean that we are comparing two real things against each other. In 1981, Stephen LaBerge of the Stanford University Sleep Research Center presented the first scientific proof that people can be awake in their dreams, aware that they are dreaming, in control of their dreams, and that they can communicate from the dream state to people in the sleep lab.

This is called "lucid dreaming," and is under intensive investigation in a great many sleep labs. This discovery demonstrates vividly that dreams can be experienced in full human Consciousness as another reality. This is probably our frontier in truth created by the Concept and Trust patterns working together.

The elements of the Trust pattern--Recognition of Experience by Intuition, creating knowing in Awareness--are not separated by anything. In this pattern, the elements are aspects of direct knowing itself. The only opportunity for something to go wrong in the process of direct knowing is the failure of Recognition to function.

Simply put, we may not pay attention to our Intuitive Experiences. We have four patterns for creating truth—Faith, Concept, Reality and Trust. Each produces truth that is acceptable to Consciousness. Whatever truth is in Consciousness is the truth we know. We know everything that we know.

If we accept what we know as the whole truth, we are overlooking the fact that truth changes, that truth is relative. The relativity of truth is in agreement with the now well- established theory of relativity produced by Albert Einstein.

Relativity theory changed time, space and matter from absolute truths to relative truths. It is not a surprise, then, to find that truth itself is relative.

In the human dimension, truth is relative to the individual human. Truth is as it Exists in human Consciousness. We can Speculate that there is such a thing as ultimate truth in Universal Consciousness.

But until we develop Reasoned Belief and direct Intuitive knowing in support of that, we must deal with what we have--the truth potential of human Consciousness. And it appears that potential includes Universal Consciousness.

Chapter 11, Understanding Belief

We have seen that Belief is formed by two processes, the Faith pattern and the Concept pattern. Faith produces Speculative Belief; Concept produces Reasoned Belief.

The Speculative Believer views Belief as absolute truth, where the Concept Believer views Belief as the best that can be arrived at for the present. These are generalizations, of course, and refer to the final and most exhaustive effort in each pattern, reflecting the maximum potential of each pattern.

We now look at Speculative Belief in greater depth. Eric Hoffer, in *The True Believer*, (his term for our Speculative Believer) says: "The facts on which the true believer bases his conclusions must not be derived from his experience or observation but from holy writ. So tenaciously should we cling to the world revealed by the Gospel, that were I to see all the Angels of Heaven coming down to me to tell me something different, not only would I not be tempted to doubt a single syllable, but I would shut my eyes and stop my ears, for they would not deserve to be either seen or heard. [Luther, "Table Talk," Number 1687]

"To rely on the evidence of the senses and of reason is heresy and treason.

"It is startling to realize how much unbelief is necessary to make belief possible. What we know as blind faith is sustained by innumerable unbeliefs. The fanatical Japanese in Brazil refused to believe for years the evidence of Japan's defeat. The fanatical Communist refuses to believe any unfavorable report or evidence about Russia, nor will he be disillusioned by seeing with his own eyes the cruel misery inside the Soviet promised land.

"It is the true believer's ability to 'shut his eyes and stop his ears' to facts that do not deserve to be either seen or heard which is the source of his unequaled fortitude and constancy. He cannot be frightened by danger nor disheartened by obstacle nor baffled by contradictions because he denies their existence." [1951]

Hoffer's description identifies the person who relies primarily--as much as possible, in fact--on the Faith pattern for creating truth. He points out that the Speculative Believer ignores evidence of the Senses and of Reason, which we are calling the patterns of Concept and Reality.

The "fortitude and constancy" he identifies as characteristic of the Speculative Believer results from knowing absolute truth. Such absolute truth varies, of course, depending on whether we are looking at the absolute truth of Hoffer's Japanese soldier, his Communist, or the Fundamentalist Christian.

This does not change its character of absoluteness, however. No Speculative Believer acknowledges any other system of absolute truth than his or her own. All other absolute truths are seen as false. Hoffer points out, "...in order to be effective a doctrine [dogma] must not be understood, but has to be believed in. We can be absolutely certain only about things we do not understand. A doctrine [dogma] that is understood is shorn of its strength."

In order to understand that there is a variety of absolute truths, one cannot be a Speculative Believer. The Speculative Believer is not responsive to Reason or to Sense Perception if these contradict the truth created by Faith.

That Belief creates truth is inarguable, since Belief is accepted as truth by Consciousness. Speculative Belief creates truth that is in every respect as valid to Consciousness as any other kind of truth.

There is no virtue in trying to explain to a Speculative Believer that his absolute truth is not true, because that statement is not true. The real issue is not truth, but conflict.

The absolute truth of the Speculative Believer is in conflict on a personal level with his or her Reason and Sense Perception, and on a social level with the truth of the majority community.

Our social reality in America today includes numerous small communities of Speculative Believers living in conflict with the majority community which creates truth by Reason. This conflict creates social conditions that lack harmony--to say the least about it.

Harmony would Exist if all Americans held a common truth. There is only one possible argument in favor of some specific common truth, as opposed to any other truth we could happen to agree upon, and that is the maximum truth of which humanity is capable of creating at a given time. Except for that, any truth would suffice as long as we could agree on it.

Perhaps we could all become Speculative Believers and enjoy harmonious community. This would require most Speculative Believers to agree on a different absolute truth than the one they hold, because of the variety of absolute truths that Exist among them. The evidence of this is the sheer number of these small communities, each separated from the majority community and from the other small communities by its truth.

This would also require Reasonable people to sacrifice the truth of Reason in favor of Speculative Belief. If such a sacrifice were made by everyone, it would probably result in the swift end of the civilization by starvation, since all of the science and technology- products of Reason--on which our survival depends would cease.

We cannot afford to create a harmonious community based on Speculative Belief because we have already created a majority community that depends on Reason for its survival. The chief architects of our daily reality are people of Reason who have created the systems which enable our survival according to Reason. Science and technology pervade our reality, and without them our reality would collapse.

Speculative Belief is useful, then, for creating individual and personalized truth, truth that need not refer to anything outside of the individual. Such truth ignores or reinforces against any conflict it may encounter with Reason or Sense Perception. It is not community truth.

Such truth is not far removed from insanity, although insanity can be seen to be a measure of community and nothing more. Insanity's legal definition is "any form or degree of mental derangement or unsoundness that makes a person incapable of what is regarded as normal, rational conduct or judgment."

The standards of normal, rational conduct or judgment are determined by the majority community. It is this majority that labels the Speculative Believer insane, and it does so only because such Belief leads to conduct or judgment that is not rational--not based on Reason.

It should not be overlooked that such conduct or judgment, even if insane, is based on truth. Every person behaves in accordance with his or her truth. If that truth generally coincides with the truth of the majority community, the person is regarded as normal. If it is highly individualized truth that conflicts with the truth of the majority community, the person is regarded as insane.

Normalcy by community standards is an attractive value to many people. But normalcy is of little concern to the Speculative Believer, and certainly is not a competitive attraction when compared with the rewards promised by their truth systems, rewards that may be as extravagant as unhindered Speculation allows.

If we wish to examine the possible ways by which we might encourage Speculative Believers to become

Reasoned Believers, I think it is most prudent to examine ourselves, for each of us has started life as a Speculative Believer.

The Faith pattern begins operating very early in childhood, providing us with Belief for every question that arises in our little Minds. When we are children, we see as children. As we grow, we learn to Reason, primarily through education.

This develops conflicts between our Speculative Belief and our new Reasoned Belief. How we resolve those conflicts determines which type of Belief will predominate in the creation of the truth we hold as adults. This issue of dealing with conflict in truth is of primary importance, and is discussed later.

Normally, we offer little resistance to the process of learning Reason through education. When there is resistance, it is typically an outside influence reinforcing our Speculative Belief, and not a choice that we make freely.

When such outside forces are present during our early years of learning Reason, they can damage our efforts in ways that have lasting effect. In order to help the Speculative Believer, we may have to think in terms of teaching remedial Reasoning.

It is surprising to me that some Americans fail to learn Reason during their educational process. Reason is inherent in every school subject, in the way the subject is broken down into daily units, in the way relevant Facts are assembled and processed, leading to rational conclusions.

Few people study Reason as such; it is part and parcel of anything we study. In view of the failure of many people to learn Reason, it may be necessary to consider the teaching of Reason itself in public schools.

How we resolve those conflicts determines which type of Belief will predominate in the creation of the truth we hold as adults. This issue of dealing with conflict in truth is of primary importance, and is discussed later.

Normally, we offer little resistance to the process of learning Reason through education. When there is resistance, it is typically an outside influence reinforcing our Speculative Belief, and not a choice that we make freely.

When such outside forces are present during our early years of learning Reason, they can damage our efforts in ways that have lasting effect. In order to help the Speculative Believer, we may have to think in terms of teaching remedial Reasoning.

It is surprising to me that some Americans fail to learn Reason during their educational process. Reason is inherent in every school subject, in the way the subject is broken down into daily units, in the way relevant Facts are assembled and processed, leading to rational conclusions.

Few people study Reason as such; it is part and parcel of anything we study. In view of the failure of many people to learn Reason, it may be necessary to consider the teaching of Reason itself in public schools.

Chapter 12, The Promise of the Patterns

There is very substantial agreement between physicists and mystics. A remarkable thing happens as a result. The mystic has a well-developed Trust pattern. The physicist has a well-developed Concept pattern.

The mystic will be able to develop a complete balance of truth in Consciousness by developing in himself what the physicist knows. His Consciousness will receive Reasoned Belief that is in very substantial agreement with what it has from Intuitive Recognition. There will be almost no conflict. The truth is not confused. The truth is about the most fundamental question people have--the nature of reality, God.

Likewise, the physicist, emboldened by his discoveries, may pursue mysticism with the same result. These become people in possession of maximum truth. Their truths agree on the maximum truth.

I think this is an ideal point of bonding for the community. By bonding on such a foundational level, we can still be free to be ourselves, directly knowing that at root we are all working together.

This possession of maximum truth today can be developed by approaching it directly. In the case of physics, it is only necessary to study the progress of physics during this century and to follow it through to its conclusions. Some excellent books have been written for the layperson.

In the case of direct knowing, it has been reported that some lucid dreamers are able to Experience enlightenment--communion with God. Lucid dreaming can be learned directly by lessons and practice, and lead to such communion. Also, there are numerous other techniques available.

This work on oneself--developing the Concept and Trust patterns--can be taken on as a part of daily living, perhaps devoting one evening a week to it. That places it within the ready grasp of almost every American. All we need are teachers.

The development of maximum truth can be a short-term personal goal, involving perhaps a number of months. For others years may be required. People have varying amounts of balance in their creative patterns, and development also depends on what changes the person wishes to make.

The process involves identifying the conflicts that currently are present and selecting a conflict to resolve. This applies to both Belief and Experience. Resolutions are in the direction of the adult patterns. As both Reasoned Fact and Intuitive Recognition increase and conflict is resolved, one grows toward the state of having rational knowledge of God in balance with one's own Experience of God by direct knowing--maximum truth.

Chapter 13, The Balance of Knowing

The Trust pattern produces experience that is direct knowing. Direct knowing shows itself in the certainty we have about our own existence.

Direct knowing is our finest creation of truth. It is not limited to mere ideas about truth, nor is it subject to the complex and suspect process of Sense Perception. It has a crystal clarity that is unique.

The typical American male has his attention heavily invested in the Concept pattern, where Reason dominates. He has not placed such emphasis on the Trust pattern, where Intuition dominates. In fact, he often resolves conflicts between Intuition and Reason in favor of Reason, choosing a course of action because it is Reasonable even though he may "know" better.

Women are reputed to have more of their attention in the Trust pattern. This has nothing to do with gender; this results only from living in a paternalistic society where the community creations have largely been the responsibility of men.

Consciousness has no gender. Yet, to the extent that the American society has any balance at all between Reason and Intuition, it is mostly a balance between the genders and too infrequently a balance within individuals.

We have looked at each of the creative patterns separately. Now that we are acquainted with them, we need to think of them as patterns to be balanced within the individual.

Establishing balance among the patterns within oneself requires deliberate management. While balance is a natural tendency, we seldom allow balance to occur on its own. Our management tends to be focused on a selection of the patterns instead of a balance among them.

Balance is established by directing attention into the various patterns. We have noted that the typical American male has most of his attention in the Concept pattern. Such a person can improve his balance by placing more attention in the Trust pattern.

The two childhood patterns have important contributions to offer toward balance. The Faith pattern produces Speculative Belief only because so much attention is placed in that pattern. Less attention in the Faith pattern generates Speculation without conclusions--imagination. This provides the Concept pattern with a fertile bed of possibilities to process.

The Reality pattern produces Sense Perception of objective reality only because so much attention is placed in that pattern. With less attention, the Reality pattern generates Experience that can be enjoyed, taken more lightly and playfully.

So many people experience objective reality as burdensome, as trial and tribulation, as suffering. This is the result of placing too much attention in this pattern. Less attention makes objective reality less real, something to be taken less seriously. Reality then becomes fun, creative opportunity abounds, and the feeling from participating in objective reality is joyful.

Balance becomes a matter of withdrawing excessive attention from the childhood patterns and placing it in the adult patterns. This creates an overall truth cycle that includes fertile imagination from the Faith pattern, the power to create Belief in the Concept pattern, the ability to enjoy the reality of created Belief in the Reality pattern, and the anchor of directly knowing how it all works from the Trust pattern.

A well-balanced person is able to imagine wonderful things, create some of those wonderful things as Reasoned Belief that becomes Reality, enjoy the Reality without feeling burdened by it, and understand that this is all happening in Consciousness as part of the creative process of Universal Consciousness.

In the Trust pattern, Conscious Awareness is directly Experiencing Intuitive Recognition. Because this is an adult process, it must be developed, just as Reason has to be developed. Reason and Intuition are not the gifts of childhood; they are the developed abilities of adults.

Can direct knowing be consensual? If Intuitive Recognition can result in shared Experience, then it can contribute to community.

Earlier, I used the example of dreaming. There is much about dream reality that is already consensual.

We all agree that time can go along normally for a while and then make a leap. We all agree that geographical space can be stable for a while and then change to some distant scene. Among those who have Experienced flying in dreams, there are a certain several ways of flying. And we agree that matter in dreams can be solid for a while, only to transform or vanish.

Physics has determined that matter is nonmaterial, that it is interchangeable with energy, and that at its root it is neither material nor energy but is ordered, instantaneously interacting patterns only. Physics has determined that time and space are relative concepts, that they are essentially fluid.

The reality that physics describes applies much better to dream reality than it does to material reality. It appears that we are in the early stages of creating a Reasoned commu nity consensus about dream reality. If this much is possible already, we can expect, especially at the swift pace with which science is moving, a much broader base of consensus within our lifetimes.

This promise is gratifying, yet, this potential for community consensus of Intuitive Recognition only equals what Reason has accomplished for Sense Perception. There are strong hints that Intuition may also possess a unique additional potential--the potential for actual shared Consciousness.

Sharing Consciousness would provide consensus of Experience, and not just consensus of ideas about Experience. Two people could actually have the same Experience and be Aware of the other's Experience as if it were his or her own. Perhaps this can be extended to the entire community, a true consensus based on mutual Awareness of Experience, not subject to disagreement because of its absolute certainty by direct knowing.

Although this ability would have to be developed in individuals one at a time, it is possible to do so; and given our excellent mass communication systems it is possible to do it for our entire society, and create an America that agrees on maximum truth by direct knowing, an America free of conflict.

Telepathy has been researched to the extent that it is now acceptable as Fact. Telepathy provides just such a link between the Consciousnesses of two people. Telepathy can be developed in the ordinary way that any skill can be developed, with learning and practice, although at this time teachers are few.

Further, it appears to me that we already have considerable telepathic Experience that we do not Recognize. I am thinking of instances where few words are needed to establish communication and mutual understanding.

Observation can make us Aware that the verbal communication itself in such instances is grossly inadequate for establishing the degree of communication that occurs. Telepathy can enable us to learn about the truths in other people's minds, broadening our outlook on truth.

Since it is an Intuitive function, telepathy tunes in to other people's direct knowing Experience. It is not correct to think that telepathy can tune into the rational thought process. Thoughts are in the Faith and Concept patterns, and telepathy is in the Trust pattern.

Likewise, it is not correct to think that telepathy can tune into one's Sense Perception, for that too is a different pattern. It is only one's direct knowing through Intuition that can be tuned into. A telepathic community would consist of people who have a great measure of privacy--complete privacy of what goes on in the Faith, Concept and Reality patterns. Individual experience is preserved to the individual.

Since telepathy is an Intuitive function, the area of shared experience is in the Trust pattern, the area of direct knowing. There is no need for privacy in this area, since anything that can be known directly is known the same way to everyone who knows it.

There is great reason for not having privacy in the area of direct knowing, because it is wonderful to acquire direct knowing immediately from people who have had to invest significant time and effort to develop it.

Experience by direct knowing lends itself perfectly to sharing. It can be compared to a community assembling a jigsaw puzzle. Each person knows a few of the pieces and doesn't mind sharing what he or she knows for the sake of helping to find out what the puzzle looks like when it is all put together.

Interesting discoveries are being made which may provide us with efficient techniques for developing shared Awareness. Dreamwork books seem invariably to include accounts of shared dreams,

dreams which are Experienced by two people who are both able to confirm that they were in the same dream together. Shared dreaming appears to be a definite possible technique for sharing Experience with another Consciousness.

Although this example does not imply Aware sharing, the question of whether telepathy can be developed for use in the dream state is under serious investigation. These areas of inquiry fall into the field of Psi research, a scientific field barely fifty years old, but which has already produced fascinating and promising results.

There exists today a considerable amount of Psi research results to study, including specific techniques for developing Recognition. Intuitive Experience is lost if it is not Recognized. Many people think they have few Intuitive Experiences, but it is only their lack of skill in focusing Recognition on Experience that deprives them.

Many new techniques have emerged specifically for developing that skill. Psychophysiology, which includes the laboratory study of dreams, has now established firmly the phenomenon called lucid dreaming. The lucid dreamer is in control of his or her dreams and can shape dream reality in any way desired.

Development of Recognition produces the skill that enables a dreamer to become lucid. Recognition, acknowledgment, is placing one's attention upon the Experience. Without that attention, the Experience never reaches Awareness.

Of greatly renewed interest, since the recent discoveries in physics, is the Experience of communion with God which has been reported throughout time by mystics. Because of the direct parallels between the physical and mystical concepts of the nature of reality, physicists are investigating mysticism, and mystics are investigating physics.

They agree that it is a nonmaterial universe. They agree that the universe is an all-encompassing entity that is made of patterns of activity (descriptions of mystics on this point vary widely because these patterns are indescribably complex). They agree that this entity creates the universe. And they agree that this entity is Conscious, based on its ability to communicate between parts of itself faster than the speed of light.

Chapter 14, Turning on the Energy

The Three Peaks model shows how truth is created. There are four creative patterns, each creating a different kind of truth. The four patterns account for every type of truth possible, except the truth about nothing and we are not concerned with nothing.

Within each pattern, there is a range within which the process operates. In the Faith pattern the range is from Information to dogma. In the Concept pattern, the range is from doubt to conviction. In the Reality pattern, the range is from detachment to immersion; and in the Trust pattern the range is from ignorance to knowing.

These patterns are not operating without control. It is not the result of chance that certain Information becomes dogma, creating a certain Speculative Belief that is accepted by Consciousness as truth. The control that exists over how these patterns perform is our own--it is our ability to place our attention where we wish.

This is the notorious "free will" which is still so much debated, the ability to choose what one will pay attention to. Attention is Consciousness itself. But it is limited deliberately so that it may gain a limited Awareness that makes it possible to focus on isolated things rather than be simultaneously Aware of everything at once (omniscient).

Attention is directed Consciousness. It is Consciousness observing directly, as if through a cylinder. Attention is what makes the human condition possible. It defines the human condition as one in which Consciousness Experiences limitations. The only difference between the human condition and Universal Consciousness is this limitation on Consciousness.

It is this limitation that creates our material world. Universal Consciousness knows everything all at once, and knows that material reality is one of its creations, created in Consciousness from Consciousness.

By Experiencing limits, we are able to examine things individually and this gives them the appearance of solidity. We are able to examine things consecutively and this gives the appearance of time. We are able to examine things in relation to each other and this gives the appearance of space.

Take away this limitation on Consciousness and the material world becomes a collection of ideas.

Attention is the Conscious energy that causes the patterns to perform. If Attention is placed on a certain item of Information in the Faith pattern, it vitalizes the Information. The Information becomes active, alive. It is Attention that makes objective reality come alive. We cannot Experience objective reality at all if we do not place our attention on it.

Our Experience of objective reality is so engrossing because we invest our Attention heavily in it. To highlight this, consider the person under hypnosis whose Attention is withdrawn from his or her body and who cannot feel pins being stuck in. This person has shifted Attention from the Reality pattern to the Trust pattern.

Attention is substantially deprived of the body and the body's Senses become largely inoperative. Attention is guided by the truth that Exists in Consciousness.

Attention travels more or less freely. It encounters difficulty when it encounters conflict, as truth is confused at that point. Attention has another difficulty because there are no paths linking the patterns laterally. When Attention is to be shifted from Faith to Concept, for example, technique is required because of the lack of a pathway.

The same applies to the shift from Reality to Trust. Technique is needed to withdraw Attention from one pattern to another along the pathways that do exist. What appears to be a lateral shift is a withdrawal from one pattern and entry into another. This requires the Attention to return to the Peaks involved.

A lateral shift--again, this is not a literal lateral-- between the Faith pattern and the Concept pattern requires the Attention to withdraw to Mind. A lateral shift from Concept to Trust requires withdrawal to Consciousness, a greater task.

Attention flows readily along any of the pathways shown on the Three Peaks model. It must make decisions, unless you make them, when it reaches the

Peak at Mind and Awareness, and again at whichever Peak it arrives at next, in the patterns. These are the Three Peaks.

Attention is not entirely in one place at a time. Every pattern requires a sustaining amount of Attention at all times. But we can be Aware of the mass of it as it travels the Three Peaks pathways.

Tracking and observing this flow of the Attention is the fundamental skill. It is simple to become Aware of Attention, but maintaining that Awareness long enough for tracking its moves is a matter that requires work.

It is Attention that energizes the elements, of those available in the patterns, for truth creation. The act itself--paying Attention--is the energizing act because it brings an element into Conscious Awareness. In Consciousness, it becomes Conscious--it Exists.

We can learn to control and direct this selection process, creating truth as we wish it to be. Left to its own direction, Attention makes its selections according to the truth that Exists in Consciousness and in response to conflict. Left to its own, it will use the truth that has been created during childhood.

There is no force that makes using free will mandatory. Some people manage to live without using it at all. It is only by the deliberate choice of the adult that the Attention is brought under personal control.

Control of the Attention, then, is the key to everything. It is the single skill that accomplishes everything. By freely choosing where to focus Attention, one freely chooses which elements will become Conscious, become truth, become reality.

A balanced person will live life knowing that it is a cooperative creation. By exercising control over Attention, a balanced person can choose where to place his Attention in society. The choice is like a vote, because wherever the Attention is placed, that is what will come to life.

Most of us have jobs. Did Attention choose the job we have on its own, using childhood patterns? Or did we make a Conscious choice to work cooperatively on some activity that we would personally like to see come to life in society? I think most people take the job that Attention hands them.

Attention may be using a childhood truth like, "My father worked in a factory, so I will work in a factory." Or a childhood truth like, "What's important is making money for myself, and I don't care what happens to other people." Adult choices that are in cooperation with the community might be, "I'd like to help the community solve its pollution problem" or "I'd like to work for a company that creates mass transit systems." We get a paycheck either way.

Chapter 15, The Resolution of Conflict

The prime purpose of identifying conflicts and resolving them is to establish balance in our creative patterns. Imbalance itself creates conflict. Too much of any single pattern creates conflict with the other patterns.

I am convinced from my own explorations in my Conciousness that conflict in truth is our greatest handicap. It is conflict that prevents the Attention from flowing smoothly through the creative patterns. It is conflict that stalls Consciousness into ambivalence as we watch our lives flow through our hands. It is conflict that robs us of creative energy and self-confidence.

Conflict can inflict, with mental torture and agony. Outside as well, conflict tears at the community, conflict that originates in individuals. Conflict is invariably a conflict in truth. There are no other conflicts than this.

The resolution of conflict is each person's task of paramount importance. The absence of conflict is harmony and peace, and a buoyant freedom to create cooperatively.

Attention is badly misused. When a conflict exists between, say, the Faith and Concept patterns, the alternative to resolving the conflict is to reinforce the threatened Faith concept with Attention. Reinforcement only escalates the conflict, and for that reason is a misuse. There is no growth represented in such reinforcement.

Growth is attained through resolution of the conflict in favor of the adult pattern. Escalation of conflict in truth poses a serious social problem. There are probably many individuals Experiencing highly escalated conflicts. I am thinking of people who face increasing conflict daily from our rapidly changing science-shaped world and who devote increasing amounts of their time and Attention to reinforcement of their conflicting Faith patterns.

Escalated conflict can burn people out. It can create serious mental problems for them. It is probably a concern of epidemic proportions. Many Speculative Believers are taught that they should not try to control their Attention, because of the risk of endangering their faith by exposure to conflicting Reason and Experience.

I have heard Attention called "the devil." That acknowledges its power, but places that power beyond personal control. It also characterizes the power in a negative way, when the power is neither positive nor negative except as it is used. It also makes the power fearsome, which is true only when we do not control it and it operates according to our childhood truths.

When we become Aware of our Attention, we see that it is at work. By identifying whether or not it is reinforcing a childhood pattern, we can spot conflicts awaiting resolution. This is one technique for identifying conflicts.

If we observe that our Attention is intensely occupied in reinforcing a dogmatic Belief, we know that the Belief is experiencing conflict; otherwise, it would not need reinforcement. Dogmatic Belief cannot help running into conflict. It is individualized and lacks consensus from the community.

Any exposure of a dogmatic Belief to the community will generate conflict. Such Believers know full well that they are experiencing conflict. But their Attention works on reinforcing the Belief rather than resolving the conflict. For such people, it is more important to be right, to have absolute truth, than it is to have harmony with others.

They may have a tendency to blame other people for the absence of harmony, when the cause is their own dogmatism. They need to see that their alienation is caused by their Belief, not by other people.

The appearance of Attention is similar whether it is reinforcing a childhood pattern or developing an adult pattern. It is important to identify the pattern involved before deciding that a conflict exists.

Tremendous amounts of Attention can be dedicated to the creation of a Reasoned Belief. Because this is happening in cooperation with the community, it is fully acceptable to the community.

An excellent example is the Reasoned Belief, "I am a college graduate." This generally requires a person to create in detail a four-year-long unfolding that appears to be self-oriented, and which removes the person for that time from the community of active co-creators of ordinary reality.

But being a college graduate has importance only within the community. The four-year absence from the active community is well-tolerated because it is viewed as an investment in the community, an investment that will produce a co-creater with advanced skills. Such a co-creator is worth waiting for.

The dedication of Attention to the pursuit of such a goal, then, does not create conflict with the community. It will create conflict with the Faith pattern, but the resolution process becomes routine in this case. With Attention focused in the Concept pattern, it withdraws from the Faith pattern and Speculative Beliefs lose vitality.

Conflict is readily apparent in ambivalence. Some introspection can often reveal the components of the conflict. Ambivalence is frequently a conflict in truth between a childhood pattern and an adult pattern, most frequently between the Faith and Concept patterns.

Ambivalence is an opportunity for growth, an opportunity to strengthen the adult pattern. By identifying the truths that are in conflict, one can resolve ambivalence by choosing the adult truth.

Self-confidence may be the issue in conflict. We may have some childhood ideas about what we are able to do, and these are in conflict with what we want to attempt as adults. Our childhood truths about ourselves may tell us that we can't do something. Our adult truths tell us we can.

Suppose you are ambivalent about moving from Chicago to New Orleans. Your childhood truths say that family is important, that you should stay in Chicago near your family. Your adult truths tell you that you are not a child any longer and that you should live your life in fulfillment of your own goals.

If the Faith pattern wins, you will stay in Chicago, and you will experience continuing conflict from your Concept pattern. If the Concept pattern wins, resolution in favor of the adult pattern, you will move to New Orleans and fulfill yourself. You may miss your family, but this childhood truth will gradually lose vitality as you focus your attention in the Concept pattern.

Conflict can be identified by looking for it, looking for a conflict that is likely to be there based on one's self-knowledge. If you want to be an artist, for example, but you can't seem to get around to it, you are experiencing conflict in truth.

You can identify the conflict by looking for it specifically. It may not be visible at first, but when you know you are looking for conflict that has certain results, it makes it possible to find the conflict. You may believe that you can never succeed as an artist, based on a truth created by some harsh criticism of your early attempts at art work during childhood. Once you identify such a childhood truth, you can weaken its vitality by deliberately withdrawing Attention from it and placing Attention on the adult pattern where you have your truth that you are an artist.

In general, conflict is resolved by shifting the Attention laterally, from the childhood pattern to the adult pattern. There is a variety of techniques for accomplishing this, including numerous psychotherapies.

The resolution of conflict is the immediate as well as the ultimate personal benefit gained from understanding the Three Peaks model. As this benefit is obtained by individuals, community increases. As it continues and enables people to achieve maximum truth, the New Age community of shared Awareness is established.

Conflict resolution is made possible by the skill of Consciously directing the flow of Attention. Reality is what is in Consciousness, and what is in Consciousness results from what Consciousness pays Attention to.

Attention vitalizes what it observes and leaves dead that which it does not observe. The skill of directing the Attention, however, is dependent on the resolution of conflict.

Conflict is what prevents Attention from flowing freely through the four creative patterns. We will find that by resolving conflict, Attention flows more freely, and that what we are calling the development of a skill is actually something we already have.

We can control the flow of our Attention now, except that our control is decreased by conflict. Many of us are so filled with conflict that we find it difficult to

Experience any control over Attention at all. The starting point is the resolution of conflict. As this proceeds, Attention will be liberated.

With freely flowing Attention, we become master creators of reality in all dimensions. The lives we Experience in ordinary reality are the lives we intend for ourselves; they conform to the truths we have created by choice.

More importantly, our access to direct knowing is unimpeded. We can know anything and know it with the unquestionable certainty of direct observation. We can settle life's most disturbing questions--who are we, what is our purpose, where do we fit into this universe, what is God, what is our relationship to God. Once we settle such questions, we have a common experience to share with others who have done the same. We share maximum truth.

This sharing occurs both in Reason and in Intuition; we share the ideas about it, and we share the Experience itself telepathically. We Recognize ourselves as co-creators in good standing, as fundamental parts of the universe in which no part is any more fundamental than another, nor any less.

www.ingramcontent.com/pod-product-compliance
Lightning Source LLC
LaVergne TN
LVHW011214080426
835508LV00007B/777